PRAISE FOR
BEYOND FAIR CHASE

"Congratulations on an approach that is fresh, clear and goes well beyond the sort of 'minimalist' discussions of hunting ethics that I've seen all too often in the past!

"You've confirmed my feelings that you're saying the kind of things I believe in and that thousands of thoughtful hunters all over the country believe in. I also have found these views strike such a responsive chord with thoughtful non-hunters that I am convinced they are in fact the kind of views that we need to advocate to insure the future of hunting and the opportunity to practice conservation of our wild resources."

**Bill Howard, Executive Vice President,
National Wildlife Federation**

"Your short essay includes an enormous amount of valuable information and makes a group of interconnected recommendations that heretofore has not been suggested to the American hunter by any organized group. You should be commended."

**Ted Kerasote, author of
*Bloodties—Nature, Culture, and the Hunt***

"Jim Posewitz has laid out, clearly and decisively, what may be the deciding factor as to whether hunting will (or should) remain a part of American culture. In the code of ethics surrounding hunting is its essence— its reason for inclusion in our cultural fabric.

"What are 'the ethics of hunting?' Why is attention to dramatic improvement in the application needed? How can that be achieved?

"Jim Posewitz answers those questions in an entertaining and insightful manner. As a hunter and a conservationist I say—it's about time."
Jack Ward Thomas, Chief, USDA Forest Service

"I know that I would have wanted this book as a young kid learning about hunting....It would have been a cherished addition, and I'm sure I would have held onto it as an adult."
Jody W. Enck, Research Specialist, Cornell University

"You've done a remarkable job of condensing and interconnecting vital concepts which must be addressed and internalized if we are to maintain our hunting heritage. Congratulations."
Holt Bodinson, Director, International Wildlife Museum, Safari Club International

"*Beyond Fair Chase* is a most important contribution to the American conservation mission. Your fine thoughts are, like those of Aldo Leopold, statements of fact about the critical role the hunting tradition plays in habitat protection. Without hunting, we North Americans would not have the passion for the land that is vital to its preservation. Those who fight to enhance the quality of hunting—as you do through *Beyond Fair Chase*—are the soul of the conservation movement."

Jack Lorenz, Director, American Land Ethics Project, The Izaak Walton League of America

"This book is timely, a tremendous contribution to the contemporary literature on the issue of hunting. It is inspiring and if all hunters would read, understand, and aspire to the ethical ideals put forth in this book, hunting will be a part of the American social landscape for many years to come."

William A. Molini, Administrator, Nevada Division of Wildlife

"I am elated about the potential uses of this marvelous book. It is a much needed tool that is long overdue."

John M. Wrede, Wildlife Conservation Officer, South Dakota Department of Game, Fish and Parks

" Jim Posewitz goes a long way toward helping hunters forge deeper relationships with the land, the wildlife it supports and the outdoor experience."

Bob Munson, Executive Director,
Rocky Mountain Elk Foundation

"You have accomplished putting together an extraordinary gold mine in *Beyond Fair Chase*. I was so engrossed with the contents I could not put the book down until I had read it completely. My impression as I finished reading the prophetic wisdom contained in this marvelous milestone is 'Actions now speak louder than words.' Translating the written composition bound in the pages of *Beyond Fair Chase* into honest visible ACTIONS of any person who desires to hunt (or hunter) is *essential* to promoting a renewed understanding of hunting and wildlife management and the preservation of the tradition and heritage of hunting."

Clair L. Huff, Executive Vice President,
Hunter Education Association

"This book is what hunting needs—now!."

Patrick J. Graham, Director,
Montana Department of Fish, Wildlife & Parks

ACKNOWLEDGMENTS

The draft manuscript of *Beyond Fair Chase* was submitted for a technical review by individuals associated with the following organizations:

> National Wildlife Federation
> Wildlife Management Institute
> United Conservation Alliance
> Rocky Mountain Elk Foundation
> Arkansas Game & Fish Commission

and by the following individuals:

Ken Barrett	Ted Kerasote
Jody W. Enck	John Wrede
	Dr. Valerius Geist

The author gratefully acknowledges the advice and suggestions made by each person. All comments helped create a better manuscript. However, such review by itself does not imply endorsement of this book, and the author assumes all responsibility for the views expressed here.

This book is dedicated to the American heroes
who won our independence from kings,
to judges who ruled that wildlife and its pursuit
belonged to all of us, and to generations of hunters
who restored the wildlife abundance I knew.
It is further dedicated to Eric Posewitz,
a first son and hunter, who died too young,
and whose spirit I shall find on one final hunt
through the stellar chaos of the cosmos.

BEYOND FAIR CHASE

The Ethic and Tradition of Hunting

by
Jim Posewitz
Orion–The Hunters Institute

FALCONGUIDES ®

GUILFORD, CONNECTICUT
HELENA, MONTANA

AN IMPRINT OF THE GLOBE PEQUOT PRESS

Illustrations by Lisa Harvey

Part of the proceeds of this book go to preserve and sustain hunting.

ISBN 978-1-56044-283-7

Posewitz, Jim.
    Beyond fair chase : the ethic and tradition of hunting / by Jim
Posewitz.
      p.   cm.
    Includes bibliographical references (p.   ).
    ISBN 1-56044-302-2 (hc). -- ISBN 1-56044-283-2 (pbk.)
    1. Hunting--Moral and ethical aspects.   I. Title.   94-10052
SK36.9.P67   1994
175--dc20   CIP

Printed in Canada
First Edition / Twenty-Seventh Printing

CONTENTS

PREFACE

A Story From The Gallatin Range

The musty smell of elk hung softly in the thick forest. A slight breeze pushed it down the slope to the trailing hunters. Without a sound, the young hunter eased upward through the snowy thicket. He had often joked, with exaggerated pride, that he could "move through the country like ground fog." Now every fiber in his body was trying to make that true.

Ahead, shadowy forms of elk picked their way upward. The frosty mist of their breath hung in the air as they worked through a jumble of downed trees.

It was a perfect hideaway for elk in Montana's

Gallatin Range. The mountain was steep; it faced northeast; and it was covered with blow-down and old-growth pine that was giving way to a thick growth of spruce. Elk knew the place well, and they took shelter there, secure in the wild tangle.

The law allowed the taking of antlered bulls, and the hunter searched for antlers as he and the elk maneuvered upward, slowly pushing through thigh-deep powder snow. Then suddenly he saw it—right above him, staring straight at him—an elk, watching him! He studied the motionless face that peered through tangled timber. It was close; less than thirty yards separated them. The boy was sure he could see the base of the bull's antlers, but the heavy timber obscured everything else. The two watched each other, first caught in mutual surprise and then frozen in suspended time. The need for a decision was upon them both.

In the stillness of that silent thicket, hearts pounded and tension stretched the minutes. It was the boy's first chance to kill an elk, and years of expectation had been carried up the mountain to this moment. The elk would not move, not a twitch. The hunter needed something to reveal, to confirm without a doubt, the presence of antlers.

The boy's father shadowed the stalk, and the youth turned his head, looking to his father for verification that it was right to shoot. That slight motion broke the stalemate, and the thicket erupted as elk bolted and crashed away through the timber. In a moment, silence absorbed the hunters as the sounds of fleeing elk faded beyond the high ridge and into the frigid November evening.

❧❧❧

The memory of that hunt remains fresh. It was a great hunt, and it remains a cherished memory. The richness of the recollection comes from knowing the hunter's first concern was to do what was absolutely right. Doing right, at the critical moment, was more important than killing a fine bull elk. There was a doubt, so the boy did not shoot. In time he would realize that the hunt had already been fulfilled.

Taking an elk is exciting anytime in a hunter's life. To pass up the chance to kill your first because of a small doubt about whether or not everything is absolutely right remains the teacher's trophy. It is part of being an ethical hunter.

The epilogue to this true-life hunter's tale is that the mountain marked that day in a way only mountains, forests, marshes, woodlots, and seasoned hunters understand. In this case, a few years later, the same hunter took a good bull not far from that tangled slope. As with all game, it was a gift the land gave the hunter, and it is possible there was a connection between the elk passed by years earlier and the elk taken later. The gift of the harvested bull was deeply appreciated. However, the hunters had already been given the highest satisfaction from the snowy thicket on that other November afternoon. It was a magic moment when a young hunter and a mountain looked long into each other's eyes—and they became one.

⊰⊱⊰⊱⊰⊱

It is a curious thing that something as private, and at times as solitary, as hunting attracts the attention of so many people with different points of view. Aldo Leopold, a thoughtful person and the father of American game management, once wrote:

"A peculiar virtue in wildlife ethics is that the hunter ordinarily has no gallery to applaud or disapprove of his conduct. Whatever his acts, they are dictated by his own conscience, rather than a mob of onlookers. It is difficult to exaggerate the importance of this fact."

Today, there are many thoughtful people saying that perhaps it is time that hunting end. Many of these people are bothered by how some hunters behave. This book is about hunter behavior, or hunter ethics. Its purpose is to emphasize the hunting experience—its importance and its meaning—and to remind all hunters of their responsibility to respect and care for all wildlife.

INTRODUCTION

The most important measure of hunting success is how you feel about yourself—how you feel when you think about and plan your hunting trip, when you are hunting, when you kill, when you tell about it, and when you remember each experience.

Feeling good about yourself as a hunter depends upon several things. One of those things is how well you understand your role as a hunter. The others are how you behave as you go about the preparation, the hunt, the killing, and the activities that follow. In short, feeling good as a hunter depends on how you think, what you value, and how you conduct yourself.

This book is about values and customs of behavior that guide the actions of hunters. In other words, this book is about hunter ethics.

The ideas in this book will help you on the path of ethical hunting. The learning process will last for as long as you hunt. There will be times when the best hunter will make a mistake. You will get excited, perhaps be tired, or just make a poor decision. The important point is to always make the best of what you do, always keep trying, and always keep improving.

As time goes on, you will find your values and behavior changing. These changes will bring you greater satisfaction as you become a seasoned hunter. While no one will ever be perfect, knowing you did the best you could will help you gain the greatest satisfaction out of being a hunter.

THE PLACE OF THE HUNTER

For more than a million years our ancestors were socially organized, using tools and hunting. In North America 10,000 years ago, they hunted beaver as large as bear, ground sloths as tall as giraffes, long-horned bison, caribou, horses, musk ox, and mammoths. As recently as 300 years ago, hunting and gathering societies were common throughout the world. We are the children of these generations of hunters.

Today, most people in the world do not have the opportunity to be hunters. Chances are, they never will. How those of us who live in the United States gained this privilege is important. It is important because keeping it will depend on how you conduct yourself as a hunter and how you care for the animals you hunt. In short, it depends on your ethical behavior.

Although the United States is home to a rich mixture of people from all parts of the world as well as descendants of Native American tribes, the law that grants us the chance to be hunters had its origin in Europe. The exceptions to this are the Native Americans' rights to hunt, which are guaranteed by treaty.

When European kings ruled over land and people, they owned the wildlife, and they granted those they favored the rights to take wild game. As a result, hunting was reserved for the royalty, not the common people. When the American colonies declared their independence, many things changed, and one of those changes had to do with who had the rights to fish and wildlife.

Early in American history, the Supreme Court ruled that property that once belonged to the king had passed to all the people. This meant that wild animals in this country belonged to all the people—equally. This was an important decision. It confirmed that our privilege to hunt was gained the same way as our other basic liberties, and it led to our current system of public hunting and fishing.

As America was settled, many wildlife populations declined. Since wild animals were owned by no one in particular, people were free to kill and sell them. Regulations and limits didn't seem necessary because wildlife was so abundant. As a result, enormous numbers were killed for commercial purposes. Their hides, meat, feathers, and other parts became resources in an unregulated marketplace. It was wildlife's darkest hour, and national tragedies occurred. One example was the extinction of the passenger pigeon. Another was the tragic loss of the great bison herds.

The disaster was not restricted to the passenger pigeon and bison alone. Deer, elk, ducks, geese, fish, egrets, and all manner of fish and wildlife had commercial or subsistence value. The uncontrolled taking of wildlife went on wherever there was settlement. With the exception of isolated pockets of wild lands and remote parts of the extreme North, the loss was almost total. An awful loneliness hushed our young nation. It was at that point some Americans concluded there had to be a better way. They believed that wildlife could and should be restored and conserved. Those people were—almost without exception—hunters. They began a fish and wildlife conservation effort that restored wildlife to every state in the nation.

There are five important things to remember about your role as a hunter.

First, the opportunity and privilege to hunt is yours by virtue of your citizenship.

Second, the animals you hunt are the result of conservation efforts of recreational hunters who stopped the market hunting and commerce in wildlife.

Third, these early hunters began the restoration and conservation of wildlife that continues to this day.

Fourth, as a hunter, you have a responsibility to future generations to see to the conservation of the animals you hunt.

Fifth, you have the responsibility to be a safe and ethical hunter.

In spite of the excellent conservation record of modern hunters, some people argue that hunting should be stopped. At times their arguments are based on the behavior of hunters. To keep our opportunity to hunt, we must always remember that wildlife belongs to all the people. The future of hunting depends upon how the majority of people view hunters. These people form their opinions when they see how we hunt and how we care for, and about, wildlife.

WHAT IS AN ETHIC?

To become ethical hunters we need to understand what ethics are. Here are some general definitions:

- ✧ An ethic is a body of moral principles or values associated with a particular culture or group.
- ✧ Ethical pertains to what is right and wrong in conduct.
- ✧ Ethics are rules of conduct recognized in respect to a particular group or culture.

Using these ideas, a definition of an ethical hunter could be constructed as follows:

A person who follows all the rules of proper behavior in a way that will satisfy what society expects of him or her as a hunter.

This definition misses something. It is not good enough because it left out wildlife—the animals we hunt. Although some people may not consider wildlife a part of human culture, it is a part of the hunter's culture. Nothing is more important to hunters than the animals they hunt. To be a hunter you must, above all else, know and respect the animals and their needs. With this in mind, the definition of an ethical hunter becomes:

A person who knows and respects the animals hunted, follows the law, and behaves in a way that will satisfy what society expects of him or her as a hunter.

This definition has three main parts:

⋄ *knowing and respecting the animals*
⋄ *obeying the law, and*
⋄ *behaving in the right way.*

Each of these parts affects the way hunters think and act. Understanding these parts will provide a foundation for ethical hunting that should satisfy hunters and the society in which they live.

KNOWING AND
RESPECTING WILDLIFE

It is important to know and respect the animals you hunt. As your knowledge of, and appreciation for, all wildlife grows, your ethical decisions will come naturally.

There are codes of ethical conduct written to fit hunting situations. They are lists of things to do and not do, and many of them are included in this book. However, you can make correct ethical choices without memorizing a lot of rules. This will happen when you see yourself and wildlife as part of the same community.

Learning about wildlife must begin before your first hunt. The learning process will allow you to become a more understanding and ethical person, and it also will help you become a more successful hunter.

As you learn about animals, you will also learn that the presence of hunters in the animal's world is natural. A hunter is a predator participating in a world where predation belongs. Just as predators "belong" to the natural system, an ethical hunter also "belongs" to the natural system. That sense of belonging becomes real when you hunt.

There are two steps in learning about the animals you are going to hunt. The first is to study wildlife just as you would any academic subject. The second is to go afield and get acquainted with the animals and the places where they live. These steps are essential to becoming an ethical and successful hunter.

There is a wealth of educational material about

wildlife and hunting. Public libraries are good places to start. Outdoor magazines feature articles about game animals and hunting methods. Wildlife conservation organizations have publications filled with useful information, including stories on hunting ethics.

Going afield is the second step. While much can be learned by reading and talking with others, there is no substitute for observing animals living in the wild.

If you have participated in athletics or learned to play an instrument, you know practice is necessary. For every minute spent playing a game or performing, hours are spent getting ready. Repetitive training prepares you to do the right thing, make the right move, and to do it even when you get excited, become tired, or feel stress. To get ready to do things right, you practice, and you practice...and then you practice some more.

Hunting is not a contest or a public performance, but practice is important to hunting as well. The objective is to become familiar with the places you hunt, the animals that live there, and the way you should react in hunting situations.

We have all heard stories of hunters who suffer "buck fever." The pattern of this "fever" is that a hunter has the opportunity to shoot an animal, but in the excitement of the moment, everything goes wrong. Easy shots are missed, ammunition is unloaded without being fired, or the hunter is "frozen" as an opportunity presents itself and then vanishes. In the worst circumstance, wild shots are taken, animals are wounded, and other hunters are placed in peril. This is not a "fever" but a hunter who is not prepared. At this point the lack of preparation can result in unethical behavior.

You need to be familiar with the field, the woods, the marsh, the forest, or the mountains where you hunt. If you work hard and long at this aspect of hunting, you can *become a part* of the place you hunt. You will sense when you start to belong to the country. Go afield often enough and stay out long enough and it will happen. Little by little you will become less of an intruder. More animals will seem to show themselves to you. You are no longer a stranger in their world; you have become part of it. Many people hunt for a lifetime without learning this, and they miss the most rewarding part of being a hunter.

In this process of practicing, you will get acquainted with the land, learn about the animals, and discover the places to search when you go hunting. You will find "sign" and learn what it means. You will learn to identify different species of wildlife, a skill you must have when you hunt. At times you will watch wildlife for extended periods, and the animals will teach you about themselves.

If you have taken the time to get acquainted with the places you hunt and the animals you expect to find, you will be less likely to make a mistake. In the process, you will become an experienced hunter before you pull the trigger the first time. The greatest reward will be gaining an appreciation for all wildlife and what it needs to survive. As this appreciation grows, the chances of unethical hunting behavior diminish.

As you gain knowledge, experience, and confidence, you will feel better about yourself and your skills as an outdoor person. In the process you will see tracks, scat, marks, and other "sign" that leave you puzzled. You will see animals and plants that you don't recognize. There will always be something to learn. If you are a new hunter, finding a teacher—a mentor—may be the best thing that can happen to you. A good mentor is a person who has the skills you are trying to gain, an ethical code you admire, and who is willing to guide your learning.

For most hunters, the mentor will be a parent or relative. If you are getting into hunting on your own, finding a mentor may be difficult, but don't be discouraged. Some outdoor clubs and associations offer hunter training. Joining a local rod and gun club can offer some possibilities. If you cannot find a person, the outdoor magazines and the publications of conservation associations will help you find answers through reading about the experiences of hunters and other outdoor people.

There are times and circumstances that lead to

hunting in areas far removed from your familiar hunting grounds. In these situations, your selection of outfitters, guides, and local hunting companions is important. Make it a point to learn about the ethical reputation of the people who will take you hunting. If you have a bad experience, find new hunting partners. If you are a paying client, you have the right and responsibility to insist on ethical service.

FOLLOWING THE RULES

In pioneer America there were few restrictions on the amount and kind of wildlife that could be taken, and uncontrolled hunting and rapid settlement soon reduced wildlife populations. Shortly after the United States became a nation, hunters began making rules to regulate hunting and preserve wildlife populations.

Today, the wide-open spaces are greatly reduced, and wildlife is hunted in a regulated process. Hunting seasons and bag limits are established to allow the taking of some animals while sustaining wildlife populations. In this way hunters are allowed a harvest, and breeding populations are maintained.

The rules governing the hunting and management of most animals are made by each state. In the case of migratory animals such as waterfowl, the federal government and the states cooperate in managing the hunt. The production of wildlife depends on many factors. Some, like the weather, change from year to year. As a result, hunting regulations can and do change.

It is the responsibility of every hunter to carefully study the hunting regulations each year to learn what is permitted. Never rely on another person to know the seasons, bag limits, and shooting hours. Even when hunting with parents, relatives, guides, or hunting buddies, the responsibility for knowing the rules is always yours. The time will come when you will be alone when you have an opportunity to shoot an animal. At that time, if you are the least bit unsure about the regulations, there is no ethical choice other than to let the animal pass.

There will be times when you see a violation or make a mistake. It is not a perfect world and violations occur. It is the responsibility of the ethical hunter to report infractions. If they involve a mistake that you made, the right thing to do is to report it. Once you do this, the peace of mind is worth whatever penalty there might be.

If you see another person doing something that appears wrong, it is your responsibility to inform someone. It is not a good idea to try to handle the situation yourself. Law enforcement requires considerable training. Even if what you see makes you angry, your job is to report it to those who are trained to handle law breakers. Many states have information "hot lines" that you can use. Learn the telephone number and carry it with you. Most important, be a good observer and take careful notes of what you see. If you have a paper and pencil, write down information, such as license plate numbers, that you might otherwise forget. Then report it as soon as you can.

Remember, ethical hunters obey the law. To violate hunting regulations is both a crime and a serious violation of hunter ethics.

THE ETHICS OF PREPARATION

Safety as a Part of Preparation

Hunter safety, a critical part of hunter education, is taught in all states and provinces. Every person who wants to become a hunter will have the opportunity or requirement to take hunter safety training. The consequences of unsafe handling of firearms or careless hunting practices can be physically and psychologically fatal. Once an arrow is loosed, or a bullet fired, no force on earth can call it back—it is final.

In our culture we are exposed to guns from childhood. The "shot heard round the world" is in our history. In our films and fantasies guns vaporize space creatures. When you become a hunter, you leave the world of make-believe for the real world. The sporting firearm you choose will be designed to kill. What it kills will be your responsibility. Habits that may have developed when guns were not real will have to die.

The ethical hunter will master the rules of firearm safety. The responsibility is personal, and it extends to insisting that those hunting with you strictly follow the rules. The following basic rules require your constant attention.

The Basic Rules of Firearms Safety
- ◇ Always point the gun in a safe direction.
- ◇ Treat every gun as if it were loaded, no exceptions.

- ❖ Store guns so they are accessible only to those permitted to use them.
- ❖ Position cased guns in vehicles so they will not move, and in a way so that other cargo will not press against a gun's sights.
- ❖ Before loading any gun, become familiar with that gun's safety features and how they work.
- ❖ If there is any question about a gun's working condition, get advice from a gunsmith.
- ❖ Keep guns unloaded until you are actively hunting in the field or in shooting position on a range.
- ❖ Keep the gun's safety in the "on" position until you are ready to shoot.
- ❖ Keep your finger off the trigger until you intend to shoot.
- ❖ Only carry and use ammunition specifically made for your gun.

- ✧ When hunting with others, agree to fields of fire, respecting each other's hunting space.
- ✧ Be absolutely sure of your target and what lies within the range of your bullet.
- ✧ Unload your gun when crossing fences or difficult terrain.
- ✧ Be sure your gun barrel is clear. If you fall, or the gun's barrel touches the ground, immediately check for obstructions.
- ✧ Do not use a telescopic sight as a substitute for binoculars.
- ✧ Protect your eyes and ears with appropriate gear.
- ✧ Never use alcohol or drugs before or while shooting.

Practice Shooting as a Part of Preparation

Shoot, shoot, shoot, and shoot some more. When the time comes to kill an animal, your responsibility is to do it efficiently. Even the best and most experienced hunters do not always achieve this objective. The ethical hunter will constantly work toward the ideal of making all shots on target and instantly fatal.

In developing your shooting skills with either a firearm or bow, there is no substitute for practice. In practice there are three objectives to keep in mind.

The first—to determine whether your firearm is shooting accurately.

The second—to learn to hit your target consistently.

The third—to develop confidence that you are going to hit where you are aiming.

Of these three, the third is often neglected. As a hunter you must have confidence that you are going to hit your target. This level of confidence can only be developed with practice. If there is doubt in your mind, it is probably going to come out the end of the barrel. When hunting, the ethical hunter squeezes the trigger to hit the animal. The ethical hunter does not pull the trigger to find out if he or she can hit the animal.

When hunting, if the first shot is a miss, and a better shooting opportunity does not present itself, do not continue firing. If you miss your best opportunity, the ethical choice is to either get a better opportunity or become a better shooter. The latter requires a return to the range. Your first shot is usually going to be your best opportunity. Make it count. Continuing to shoot at fleeing targets or groups of birds, hoping to "get lucky," is blatantly unethical. It risks crippling animals and hitting the wrong animal.

Staying proficient at shooting is a lifetime activity. The ethical hunter will constantly hone his or her shooting skill and retain his or her shooting confidence. When you squeeze the trigger, or turn loose an arrow, you must believe that you will hit where you are aiming. Only practice can build that expectation in you as a shooter.

An ethical hunter has the responsibility to know the capability of the weapon used. With firearms, you must match your gun and bullet to the game being hunted. With archery equip-

ment, you must match your bow weight and
arrow to the game hunted, and you must keep
your broadheads sharp.

Physical Fitness as a Part of Preparation

*The following discussion (and a later section on fair
chase) is directed at hunters who are not mobility
impaired. It is recognized that people who are mobility impaired need, deserve, and must be given the
opportunity to enjoy hunting.*

Hunting is a rigorous activity. One advantage
animals have is that they are perfectly attuned to
the terrain and cover that protects and provides
for them. Unfortunately, most humans are strang-

ers to wild places. Today's hunter has to learn how to function in wild country. A hefty effort is required whether you tramp through briar thickets in pursuit of cottontail rabbits or scale stony peaks in search of a mountain goat. There are physical demands to hunting; they are a part of hunting.

Just as you must prepare mentally for hunting, you must also prepare yourself physically. Some common unethical practices can be traced to people who are physically unable to persist in the hunt. For example, a person who is short of breath from hiking or climbing will not be able to hold a rifle steady and take a sure shot. A tired individual may resort to taking a marginal shot when a little more effort would have placed the hunter in a better position.

There are times when the best hunter will wound an animal. You must be physically capable of persisting in the pursuit of that animal under any circumstance. In the case of big game animals, this could call for an arduous day or more. When you prepare yourself physically for hunting, prepare for that day.

When a big game animal is taken, you will have to bring out the meat. This will be physically demanding as well.

The ethics of hunting deteriorate as machinery and modern technology are substituted for hunter stamina, skill, knowledge, and patience. The use of machinery—trucks, motorcycles, all-terrain vehicles, and other kinds of power equipment—are often at the root of ethical problems. Almost everyone is offended when machines are used to chase animals. It is contrary to the concept of hunting and is often the source of the bad image hunting suffers among landowners and the general public.

It is almost a certainty that each of us will need a machine to get to where we will hunt. However, once we get there, we must separate ourselves from the high technology world and become hunters. It is the ethical choice. Physical capabilities differ; you should evaluate yours honestly and select a hunting challenge within your ability and condition.

If you are prepared physically, you are more likely to make the right ethical choice when afield. You will also be healthier and will probably enjoy a fuller life.

There will come a time, however, when each of us must face an inevitable truth and accept personal physical limits. For all of us, wear, tear, and time will dictate that we accept limitations. It will be a phase in life to savor patiently hunting squirrels in a rural woodlot and be content with memories of stalking bighorn sheep among eagles. This will be a time to show a new facet of personal nobility by saying no to proposals to access wild country with roads even though our own time to be there may have passed. It is a commitment that we owe the hunters of tomorrow...if hunters are to have a tomorrow.

Landowner Relations as a Part of Preparation

Although wildlife belongs to all of us, opportunities to hunt occur on two types of land: private and public. How you conduct yourself while hunting is the same wherever you go, but each type of ownership has its own considerations.

Private Land

It is important to develop a positive attitude toward landowners based on respecting them as individuals. Just as ethical hunting is based on appreciating and respecting wildlife, ethical behavior on private land starts with appreciating and respecting the landowner.

When dealing with private landowners, keep in mind they are individuals. Just as you are different from other hunters, each landowner is a one-of-a-kind person. If a landowner allows you to hunt, that does not mean it is okay to cross onto the neighbor's place. If one landowner chooses to say no, that doesn't mean the next one shares that view. The key to getting along is getting to know them as individuals.

Thinking about landowners begins with the realization that, if there is wildlife on the property, it is because the landowner provides suitable habitat. At times wildlife does move onto land that is being managed for other purposes, but most landowners have wildlife on their property because they want it there. This means they provide for it, care about it, and consider its welfare in land management. Showing respect for these personal feelings is extremely important.

Plan your trip so you approach the landowners under reasonable circumstances. Contact them at reasonable times, preferably well in advance of the chosen hunting day. Let these people see you, it will help them decide if they can trust you. If you plan to hunt with a companion, bring that person along or tell the landowners the exact nature of your hunting party. Let them know you are interested in them and in being of service if you can help. Learn how to accept "no" graciously; there is always another day.

The goal is to make a friend, not just find a place to spend a day. An off-season remembrance, even if you can only afford a card, lets the person know you care. You are going to be one of many people asking to hunt; give the landowner a reason to like you.

Like firearm and bow safety, there are rules to follow to help get along with private landowners:

- ❖ Ask the landowner where he wants you to hunt, and what areas to avoid. Park your car where he tells you and leave it there.
- ❖ Respect the land as if it were your own— the golden rule works.
- ❖ Leave gates as you find them. If you have a concern over an open gate, ask the landowner before you leave.
- ❖ Hunt away from livestock and buildings.
- ❖ Stay out of fields of unharvested crops.

- ⬦ If hunting with a dog, keep it under control.
- ⬦ Thank the landowner when you are leaving, offer to share what you may have taken, and tell him of things you saw that may be of concern or interest.
- ⬦ Talk to the landowner before each hunting trip, particularly if you plan to bring someone new along.

Remember, landowners are people just like everybody else. They have good days and bad; they have problems of their own. If you can be a positive part of their life, you will have mastered the art of human relations, and of finding good places to hunt.

Behind Weathered Doors

Finding places to hunt is often difficult, but there are times when the search leads to experiences never to be forgotten. Many of these experiences begin when you knock on the weathered door of a farm or ranch house. This is the story of a young hunter who had one of those doors opened to him.

❧❧❧

The boy was a strong lad, just past his fifteenth birthday, with a passion to hunt and not much else, when he knocked on the weathered door looking for work. The old farmstead, in New York's Hudson River Valley, was good wildlife property, and the job was building fence, doing simple repairs, and caring for livestock. Wealthy people came there to hunt, but this privilege was not extended to the hired help.

The land was a mixture of early succession hardwoods, a scattering of ponds, and some swamp land connecting little patches of open water. In the fall, black ducks found the ponds, woodcock knew the swamp edges, and ruffed grouse exploded from overgrown apple orchards.

The boy enjoyed being around the farm, but he had a passion to hunt too. For him, hunting was mostly an exercise in finding a place to hunt in a valley where most of the land was posted against hunting. When he did find a place, he hunted hard for gray squirrels, rabbits, and the occasional grouse. The grouse were usually safe, untouched by the tight, full-choked shot pattern of the boy's old shotgun. Then an elderly hunter came to the farm, and the boy's life changed.

The man had hunted big game on several continents. He was a cultured connoisseur of sport and one of those classic gentleman hunters reminiscent of another time and place. When the boy met him, the old man was well into his sixth decade. The landowner instructed the young hired hand to tend to the older hunter, who was now racked by emphysema and barely able to spend a day afield. The boy became the old man's companion; it was a safety precaution, nothing more.

It didn't take long, however, for a special kinship to develop between the old hunter and the boy. For the boy, it opened up a wonderland of bird shooting with fine guns and good dogs. The man and boy were a sight together—the old man in traditional tweeds and the boy in patched jeans, a tattered hand-me-down wool jacket, and five-dollar boots from the Army-Navy store. They became a predictable sight of autumn on the farm.

The two of them laughed and wheezed their way over grasslands, through swamps, and among the hardwood thickets—one with all the vigor and stamina of a hunter in his prime, the other with just the heart.

Soon the man decided his hunting companion should have special privilege. For each trip the boy was allowed to select from the old hunter's collection of superb shotguns. The boy who just wanted any place to hunt now went afield on a rich hunting ground with high grade Parkers, elegant Purdys, and other wonderful classic doubles. So they would hunt together, the fading, hacking hunter of another time and the boy who somehow had entered a world beyond his dreams.

They hunted this way for years, the old man's maladies wearing him down to little more than a rack of bones. On their last hunt, the maturing young man drove the old hunter to the top of a long slope. Then, medication at the ready, the old man worked his shaky way downhill. His hacking cough had worsened, and after one terrible siege, he forced himself upright, shotgun at the ready, and proclaimed, "What the hell—I'm still alive." They went on.

The dogs worked superbly, and the birds flushed as if part of an orchestrated performance. Three of the four birds flushed were taken, the last one cleanly by the old gentleman. It was a good hunt, and though they both knew it would be their last together, it passed without ceremony.

The young man did not see his friend again. The memories, however, remain vivid—memories of a gentleman, a hunter, fine dogs, exciting birds, and superb guns to match the quality of the time they shared.

−<›−<›−<›

Access to land and the lives of people are part of the same circle. Few of us will enjoy the experience this young boy came upon by chance, but the possibility is there. It may be behind the next weathered door you face when you ask permission to hunt on private land.

Public Land

Ethical behavior on public land involves the same guidelines you observe on private property. The difference is that public land belongs to you and a lot of other people—all at the same time. This simplifies the issue of getting access to hunt, but it complicates the relationships between hunters and between hunters and other outdoor recreationists.

There will be circumstances when crowded public hunting areas and human nature combine to bring out the worst in people. At times a sense of competition develops in which being first to reach a patch of cover or first to take a shot replaces rational, ethical behavior. There are two ways to address ethics in these situations. One is to focus on improving the hunting ethics of the participants; the other is to create regulations and establish hunting seasons that would avoid conditions conducive to unethical behavior.

It is the responsibility of the ethical hunter to work on both solutions. You can influence the behavior of hunters around you by demonstrating ethical behavior and expressing your desire to have a pleasant hunting experience. Talk to other hunters and suggest hunting strategies that represent an honest sharing of the opportunity. Agree to fields-of-fire with hunters nearest you. If you have game in your bag, perhaps you can defer the next opportunity to someone who may not be as fortunate. Courtesy, just like rudeness, is contagious.

The kind of hunting opportunity you have on public land is governed by land and wildlife management agencies. If management practices are not producing quality hunting opportunities, you should get involved in the management process. Your access to people who make these decisions is guaranteed by law. Find out who they are and get involved; it is the American way. To magnify your voice, join a conservation organization that shares your view. Do not sit on the sideline and complain; it is a waste of time and it doesn't work.

There will be times when hunters and non-hunters are afield in a common area. Take a moment to acknowledge that you are aware of their presence. A wave of the hand takes only a moment, and a brief conversation is even better. It will show them that you are responsible and that there is no need for them to feel threatened by your presence.

⟨⟩⟨⟩⟨⟩

In this book we have discussed things to think about and do in preparation for the hunt. Prepared with this knowledge and these skills, it is now time to take it to the field, forest, woodlot, and marsh.

THE ETHICS OF THE HUNT

Fair Chase

Fundamental to ethical hunting is the idea of fair chase. This concept addresses the balance between the hunter and the hunted. It is a balance that allows hunters to occasionally succeed while animals generally avoid being taken. This would be a simple concept if it were a single hunter pursuing an animal in massive wild country. In the real world, it is a complex topic involving the entire community of hunters, populations of animals, remnants of wild land, and management agencies that define both the terms and conditions of hunting.

When the hunter with spear in hand stalked wildlife in the primal forest, the pursuit was well within the bounds of fair chase. That situation is past. Technological advancement, the human population explosion, and the loss of wild lands required a new balancing between the hunter and the hunted. Initially that balancing took the form of rationing the available wildlife through protective laws, regulations, and refuges. Habitat protection, land acquisitions, and wildlife management activities were added to bolster wildlife populations. These techniques for rationing opportunity and for maintaining the supply have sustained hunting, but they have not addressed a fair-chase relationship between the hunter and his or her quarry.

The concept of fair chase is important to hunting. The general public will not tolerate hunting under any other circumstance. Until ethical hunting environments and fair-chase principles are addressed as a part of resource management, deciding what is fair remains a personal responsibility. Although you and the animals you hunt are equally involved, only you—the hunter—can judge its fairness, and the choices you make are important because they reflect on hunting as an activity.

There are some activities that are clearly unfair as well as unethical. At the top of the list is shooting captive or domesticated big game animals in commercial killing areas where a person with a gun is guaranteed an animal to shoot. These shooting grounds are alien to any consideration of ethical hunting. When discussing the ethic of fair chase, it is important to clarify that we are talking about hunting free-ranging wild animals.

Shooting preserves where birds are put in the field present difficult ethical decisions. Ethical judgment has to be tempered by the realities of the people who use these places and the opportunities available to them. Shooting preserves protect isolated habitat that otherwise might be destroyed or developed; they provide habitat for other wildlife species; they provide opportunities for training dogs; novices can be introduced to bird shooting; and veteran hunters can maintain shooting skill. In Aldo Leopold's 1933 text *Game Management*, he states:

"...the recreational value of game is inverse to the artificiality of its origin...."

This is still a standard that can be used to measure these activities.

The mechanized pursuit of wildlife is high on the list of violating fair-chase principles. We have invented machines to carry ourselves over land, sea, and air. Evolution of the animals we pursue can not keep pace with these inventions. If we are to pursue animals fairly, the ethical choice is clear—we pursue them on foot. The ethical hunter never chases or harasses wildlife with a machine.

The ethical hunter must make many fair-chase choices. In some areas, chasing big game with dogs is an accepted custom. In other places, it is considered an unfair advantage for the hunter. Likewise, luring animals with bait or hunting in certain seasons sometimes is viewed as giving unfair advantage to the hunter. While local custom and practice need to be respected, it is equally important to be honest about the result of these practices. If there is a doubt, advantage must be given to the animal being hunted.

In addition to hunting practices, there is a constant flow of products developed to provide advantages to hunters. Sights, scents, calls, baits, decoys, devices, and techniques of infinite variety fill the marketplace. In each case an individual choice must be made as to what sustains fair chase and what violates that concept.

Hunters have experienced cases where the public has stepped in and put an end to certain hunting seasons and practices. In most cases, these challenges have addressed what is fair chase and what is not. As hunters, we must establish a high ethical standard of fair chase or we risk three things important to our future. One is the leadership in doing what is right for wildlife; the second is the opportunity to hunt; and the third is our self-respect.

Deciding to Shoot

A Story About The Bucks Of Lost Hat Pass

The camp was a long day's saddle horse ride from the trailhead. It was deep in wild country that later became part of a national wilderness called Scapegoat. The Cooney Creek campsite, buried in heavy timber at the bottom of a dark, narrow valley, didn't offer much of a view. After contemplating the location, however, you could appreciate why the outfitter selected this somewhat dismal hole as a seasonal home. A grassy slope on a side hill just above the site was good horse pasture, and the heavy old-growth timber was first-class shelter from nasty autumn storms. The timber also hid the camp from the high, sparsely timbered, rocky ridges bordering the valley.

It was those high ridges with their patchy scrub

timber, small grassy parks, and limestone out-crops that provided the promise of good hunt-ing. They caught and held the fancy of bucks and bulls, and that is why the hunters came. The lime-stone ridges grew big-antlered animals that be-came campfire tales of things real, sometimes imagined, and always exaggerated—tales of ani-mals that could only be told with arms spread and fully extended over the tale-teller's head.

Harry, one of the guides, brought his 16-year-old daughter to camp to help with the chores and learn the ways of wilderness. After a few days tending to the paying clients, Harry asked the outfitter for a little time to take his daughter on a hunt. Getting permission, they decided to head for the ridges favored by old, large mule deer.

The two left camp early and rode their horses slowly through the scattered timber and open, rocky slides that covered the steep sidehills of "Lost Hat Pass"—a descriptive but unofficial name hunters had given the windy crest. A few years earlier, a gust of wind had caught a Stetson hat and sent it off into space, never to be seen again.

Before the hunters reached the crest of the ridge, they tied their horses and went ahead on foot. The day was cool, partly cloudy, and unusually calm. Slowly, father and daughter hunted their way along the ridge.

Suddenly they dropped to the ground, both having spotted the deer. Just ahead of them, four magnificent mule deer bucks were walking off the ridge toward the scrub timber below them. It was a classic opportunity. The bucks were unaware of the hunters, crouched motionless above them. The girl studied the bucks, never lifting her rifle. She remained motionless, in awe of those magnificent animals and their sweeping antlers, bright in a hazy, midday sun.

At first it was the softest of whispers. "Shoot," advised the seasoned guide who often had been in this situation with clients. Ever so quietly, he said, "Sh... sh... shoot." "Shoot," he counseled still another time. "Shoot!" The whispered instruction increased in volume as the father tried to get his daughter to respond.

As for the hunter, she had no urge to shoot. Although it was her first opportunity to take a fine animal, she was content to just admire the bucks. One by one, they began dropping off the ridge, disappearing over the side, down into the shelter of the timber. Her contentment, however, was not reaching Harry, who decided to ask straight out, "Aren't you going to shoot?" Her calm answer, spoken for the first time, was simply, "No."

"For heaven's sake, shoot," Harry urged again. At that moment the guide was trying to help his daughter get her first deer and put one of those fine bucks on the camp's meat pole. The hunter remained content with the moment as it was, and the bucks passed.

❧❧❧

In this story, the hunter did not have "buck fever," she was just not ready to shoot one of those bucks. She did the right thing. She savored the hunting experience and let the bucks pass. The lesson is that it is up to you to decide when you are ready to kill. It may take time before you feel ready, and it is important to reserve that decision for yourself.

Since that first hunt, the girl has taken many

67

deer, elk, antelope, and upland game animals. Yet she is content with her decision that day on "Lost Hat Pass." For her, that day remains one of her fondest memories.

❧❧❧

If there is a sacred moment in the ethical pursuit of game, it is the moment you release the arrow or touch off the fatal shot. As a hunter:

- ❧ You have made a decision to kill the animal you have pursued,
- ❧ You are confident that the shot will be a good one, and
- ❧ You feel right about taking an animal you respect.

The previous passage used the word "you" five times. It emphasizes that you are the person who has to feel right about taking game when the opportunity presents itself. The lesson in the story about the girl who chose not to shoot is important. There will be a lifetime of chances to shoot game—do it when you feel right.

The idea of feeling right is something you should think about each time you have the opportunity to take an animal. You may have been hunting for years, taking game on a regular basis, when quite unexpectedly you might feel differently about shooting a particular animal. It is important to respect your feelings at that moment.

Circumstances of a hunt will affect the way you feel. A chance to take an animal may present itself after you have invested a lot of energy and skill in a hunt, and everything will feel right. On the other hand, you may encounter an animal driven to you by chance, perhaps exhausted from being chased by other hunters. The ethical thing to do may be to let it pass. The important thing is to make that decision for yourself.

For every hunter it is a good practice to let an animal that could be killed pass without harm every now and then. This is a way in which you can demonstrate to yourself what is most important about being a hunter. You don't have to do it often or all the time, but it is important to be able to do it. In this way, you will affirm that killing is only part of what is important about hunting. In addition, you might learn something about the animal's behavior by watching it long after the time you normally would have touched off the shot or sent the arrow.

After you have decided that you are ready to kill an animal, two things demand your complete attention. One is safety within the range of your gun or bow, and the other is hitting the animal with a killing shot.

In the excitement of this moment, safety still demands your attention. That attention must be directed at objects between you and the target, what is beyond the target, and the potential for ricochet. At this moment, you must recall all that you learned about shooting safety, and you must study the terrain between you and the target and beyond the target. When hunting animals that normally just jump out within range, such as game birds or cottontail

71

rabbits, you must constantly be aware of where you are and what is within range of your sporting arm.

After safety considerations are satisfied, you must concentrate on hitting the animal in a vital organ. When hunting upland game birds or waterfowl, this is a matter of being in range and putting the pattern of shot on target. For the big game hunter, it is a matter of aiming at a vital area and of being within range of your gun or bow and within the capability of your marksmanship. The most effective target area is the rib cage because it covers the vital organs.

The most common mistake is shooting at something out of range. An ethical hunter knows the effective range of his gun or bow and gives the target animal the benefit of any doubt. The "hail mary" idea of putting shot in the air and hoping for a lucky hit is unacceptable. Such a practice risks crippling, is almost never successful, and may deny an opportunity to another hunter. If a good shooting opportunity does not present itself, let the animal pass.

Wounding

It is not a perfect world and you will not always kill with the efficiency of a perfect marksman. There will be times when the first shot is not instantly fatal. When this happens, you are responsible for bringing the matter to an ethical conclusion. This means giving the wounded animal your undivided attention.

Upland bird and waterfowl hunters often hunt with dogs, and there is no greater asset in retrieving wounded game than a trained dog. Without a dog, an ethical hunter must pass up any shot where the retrieval of a dead or wounded animal might be difficult or impossible.

When a big game animal is wounded, everything about the hunt changes dramatically. The hunter, who may have been looking for any legal animal, must now find one particular animal. In addition, it is that one animal that sets the pace, direction, distance, and probably the duration of the pursuit. For the hunter, it is a time when his or her skills as a hunter, woodsman, and naturalist will be tested as well as his or her personal character.

Ethics demand that the wounded animal be pursued, found, and killed. There will be times when wounds are not fatal, and animals can and do recover. Generally, there will be no way of knowing if a wound is fatal or not, so every animal must be pursued as if it were mortally wounded.

Physical signs alone will not always lead you to the wounded animal. When such evidence fades or is lost, you will have to rely upon your knowledge of the area you hunt. Wounded animals tend to go downhill, seek water, and return to their most secure haunts. Those will be the places to carry out the search if initial tracking fails.

A Story of a Lost Bull

Persisting in the pursuit of a wounded animal is the ethical responsibility of every hunter. Every now and then you hear stories that reveal how deeply hunters feel about hunting, about the animals they hunt, and how they find ways of expressing those feelings. The following story is about a bowhunter who wounded a bull elk and about how he dealt with his responsibility to the elk and to himself.

◈◈◈

It was mid-afternoon and the bowhunter found himself working up a small knob covered with thick, second-growth lodgepole pine. The knob was part of the north slope of a larger mountain not far from the Continental Divide. Like many such slopes, this one was a good mixture of muddy wallows, dense alder thickets, and lodgepole pine tangles. The only openings in the cover were occasional rock slides and a few grassy parks and wet meadows. The place also had elk, lots of them, and they were active.

The rut was on, and although the wind was strong, the hunter could catch the smell of elk as the cows, calves, and a handful of excited bulls whistled, grunted, and snorted. The bowhunter knew the place well. In previous years he had taken elk there, and again he stalked the mountainside, listening to the elk around him. It was a technique he often used, and he preferred it to trying to call an elk with his own imitation. Stay hidden, stay quiet, stay patient, and stay with the milling elk—opportunity will present itself.

Sure enough, after a time the hunter caught a glimpse of elk legs moving through the dense cover of second-growth lodgepole. Suddenly the animal dropped its head to pass under a leaning tree, and the hunter saw the heavy rack of a fine six-point bull. Slowly, the archer drew his bow as the elk moved forward, exposing its rib cage. The arrow flashed through the space between hunter and elk and then disappeared into the bull's side. The hunter knew it was a good shot, and he knew he had killed this bull. He had done it just this way at other times.

The bull bolted with a grunt, and then, carrying itself heavily, disappeared around the curve of the hill. The hunter knew it would not go far, and he followed the bull to a small, grassy meadow. Just as expected, the bull was down, and the archer quietly retreated to let it die. Through his binoculars the hunter watched the bull as it lay, head down on the grassy hillside, obviously fatally wounded.

The other elk, unaware of the bowhunter's presence, continued their rutting activities, challenging one another for dominance. Suddenly the piercing bugle of another bull rolled down the mountainside. Almost unbelievably, the sound of that bugle apparently gave the mortally wounded elk a charge of adrenalin. The bull rose and took off in response to a challenge it had no doubt heard before. The hunter sat in stunned amazement as the bull disappeared into the timber.

The hunter had enough experience to know the wounded elk could not last long. The arrow had hit it well and disappeared into its chest. Internal bleeding was sure to drain the animal's strength, and the adrenalin rush would soon wear off. The hunter followed the bull's trail and was still tracking spots of blood and fresh tracks through heavy timber when darkness gathered and swallowed the mountain.

The next day the hunter returned and resumed

tracking. The bowhunter, certain the animal was dead, had returned to the mountain without his bow. The hunt went on as the tracker, often on hands and knees, followed the fading trail. Time was the enemy, erasing the tiny clues that might lead the hunter to his quarry. He was no longer looking for any elk; he was looking for the elk he shot. He told himself he must find that one elk or there could be no peace in his mind. There is a point in life when people make rules for themselves, and this hunter now had a new rule.

The search went on, and each new day, without exception, the hunter returned to the mountain. Word of his daily, determined pilgrimage to the high country in the face of the gathering winter began to be known. His friends tried to talk him into giving it up; a few questioned his sanity. As the searching persisted, some urged him to abandon his obsession. The animal was gone; the meat was now beyond salvage. There was no longer any point in finding the remains. There were other elk, his elk license was still valid, and there was still plenty of hunting season remaining. Yet each day he returned to the mountain, sometimes with his dog to help look for the dead bull. For this hunter, there was only one elk.

As the days passed, the search changed. Now the hunter watched the ravens, looked for the tracks of coyotes, and listened for squawking jays—all signs from scavengers that might lead him to the elk. Over and over he traversed the hillside, covering land he had covered before. He knew that somewhere up there in the gathering winter an elk lay dead and he had to find it. He promised himself that if he didn't find that bull, he would never hunt again.

Exactly thirty days after he sent an arrow into the chest of that six-point bull, the bowhunter's odyssey ended in a snowy, high-country alder thicket. He found the dead bull. Not much remained of the carcass—some hide and backbone, the scavengers had taken most of it. The skull and antlers were still there—and so was the arrow. The arrow had done what the hunter knew it would do.

The bowhunter sat a long time in the snow and thought of the many times he had passed within yards of this bull in the last thirty days. He thought of the other elk he had killed and the elk that were his constant companions throughout his solitary search in this still wild place. He thought of many things, then slowly he reached into his coat, pulled out his elk license, filled it out, and attached it to the bull.

This hunt was over. In another year, the archer would hunt again.

❧❧❧

There are many lessons in this story of a bowhunter's dedication to an animal he had wounded. The fact that the meat wasn't utilized by the hunter is unfortunate, but other animals of the forest used it all. The important point is that the hunter stayed with the hunt until he satisfied himself that it was over. He had mortally wounded an animal and did not rest until he sat with that animal. This is a profound expression of respect. He also showed consideration for other hunters when he chose not to use his elk tag on another animal. The most important lesson of this story, however, was when the hunter said later, "... within myself I knew I done right."

ETHICS AFTER THE SHOT

Accepting the Gift

Earlier in this book we said, "If there is a sacred moment in the ethical pursuit of game, it is the moment you release the arrow or touch off the fatal shot."

To this we add the idea: If there is a time for reverence in the ethical hunt, it is when you claim, or accept, what you have killed.

For a hunter, this can be the most serious and meaningful moment of the hunt. The significance is the same whether you are claiming a grizzly bear in the wildest country left on earth, a cottontail rabbit in a tiny woodlot, or a duck from a wet retriever that is shaking from its own excitement of the moment.

What you have before you is a wild animal, and it is the product of many things. It is an appropriate time to pause and appreciate what has just taken place. You have taken an animal in a hunt. It has come to you:

- ◇ through the land and the trials of natural selection,
- ◇ through the efforts of people who protected your opportunity to hunt,
- ◇ through conservation programs that restored wildlife to a depleted land,
- ◇ through land management efforts that protected the place where you stand,
- ◇ through wildlife management programs that insure wildlife harvest is balanced with wildlife production, and

✧ through those people who taught you to hunt and to hunt safely.

The animal lying at your feet or resting in your hand contains all of these things. If any one of them were missing, or were to disappear, you would be standing alone and both your heart and your hand might be empty.

This animal that is now yours is the product of centuries of natural evolution. It is also the product of the more recent evolution of hunting and wildlife management in this country. In this way it represents:

✧ the exuberance of former President Theodore Roosevelt who campaigned for the preservation of wildlife,

- ✧ the boundless energy of forester Bob Marshall, who argued for preserving the wilderness,
- ✧ the thought of biologist Aldo Leopold, father of wildlife management, who articulated a beautiful hunting philosophy, and
- ✧ above all else, the work of generations of hunters who would not let these animals and the places they need be destroyed.

There is a lot to think about and be thankful for. It is well to think of these things when you anticipate hunting, now and then when you are hunting, and always when you claim an animal that is, in so many ways, a precious gift. It is a gift that comes to you from ancestral hunters in the caves of our origins, from native hunters of all lands, from those who won our independence

from kings, from our nation's first conservationists, and from all those who work to protect wild
places and the wildlife that lives there. Most of all,
it is a gift that comes from the land. Appreciate it.

Care and Beyond

One of the primary purposes of hunting is to
exercise our need to remain a part of the natural
world. We still have the desire to participate in
the natural process. Our developed world is becoming separated from nature; it is becoming ar-
tificial. Even the outdoors is often delivered
through the window of a tour bus or processed
through movies, videos, and theme parks that
mock reality. Hunting is one of the last ways we

have to exercise our passion to belong to the earth, to be part of the natural world, to participate in the ecological drama, and to nurture the ember of wildness within ourselves.

In the beginning, humans hunted to live. Today some still live to hunt. Originally it was a matter of survival to utilize what was killed. Today, using what is killed is essential to ethical hunting.

After you have taken possession of the animal you have killed and taken time to appreciate it, it is then time to care for your gift. The task at hand will vary. For some animals it is simply a matter of putting it into your game pouch and continuing. For big game there is field dressing and properly caring for all the useable parts.

Under all circumstances, the ethical hunter cares for harvested game in a respectful manner, leaving no waste. Field dressing has several advantages. It reduces the risk of spoiling edible parts, and it returns parts of the animal to the earth where it found life.

Field dressing begins the natural recycling process that involves scavenging birds, insects, and decay as the unused parts return to the energy and nutrient cycles of the ecosystem. This is a marvelous process of renewal, and surplus parts of what you harvest (the entrails, for example) should be thoughtfully returned to the earth. If you hunt in populated areas, a different method of disposal may be required.

Harvested game will usually be taken from the field to the hunter's residence. As in all aspects of the hunt, it remains critical to show respect for the animal taken. In transporting dead animals it is also a time to be sensitive to the feelings of other people, many who do not hunt, and some who are critical of hunting. Any dead animal in transport should be discreetly covered. If the body cavity of a big game animal needs to be exposed to cool, then at least cover its head. Yes, the antlers too. Although taking a fine animal may make you feel proud, displaying it to strangers will cause more bad feelings than good. In addition, take big game straight home and hang it out of sight. Avoid stopping along the way, even if it is the local custom.

At some point the animal will be butchered, cooked, and eaten. Feathers, hide, head, feet, bones, and such will be left at each step in processing. The rule of respect still applies to their disposal. Ideally, the remains of game will not end up in a garbage can, trash bin, or an urban landfill—it is disrespectful. It is also ugly, and it upsets people who see it. While it is not necessary to go to extremes on this point, try to take the remains of game animals back to the forest or field. This step is not critical to ecosystem health, but it does represent a persistent commitment to respectful treatment of game. It is also a good idea to place these items away from roadsides and other common areas so other people do not see them and so scavenging animals are not attracted to these areas.

The Notion of Trophy

Trophy animals have held the attention of hunting cultures since images were painted on pyramid walls and antlers were hung in medieval castles. Today, the sight of a heavy-antlered buck streaking through the autumn brush is just plain exciting. No matter how long you hunt or how many deer you look at, there is always a thrill when you encounter these animals. Their images adorn our literature; their reality stalks our experiences; their myths tease our expectations.

The idea of killing an animal just because it is exceptional is also a common criticism of hunters and hunting. It is argued that the best of a species should be protected, not pursued. As ethical hunters, how we deal with the idea of pursuing, taking, and living with trophy animals is important to ourselves and our future. Above all, we should realize that any animal taken by ethical hunting is a trophy.

Biologically, the most vital animals in a wildlife population are the productive females. The females produce the young, protect them when they are most vulnerable, and teach them how to use the country in order to survive. From the point of view of a subsistence hunter, a yearling, female animal may be the most tender and palatable, and generally the preferred meat.

The idea of trophy probably came from Europe along with other values and customs brought by the new immigrants. The taking of older, well antlered, or large game animals has been viewed as a measure of the ability of the hunter. The assumption is that the animal had survived many hunts because it possessed superior survival skills. Thus it would follow that the hunter who took this animal was also superior. To a large extent, taking an exceptional animal is still a motivating influence and that is not likely to change. As ethical hunters we must address:

⬦ what we consider a trophy animal, and
⬦ why we pursue a trophy animal.

If done with understanding and sensitivity, trophy hunting can fall within the definition of ethical hunting.

What Constitutes a Trophy Animal?

The basic idea of a trophy is the pursuit of an animal that has grown to maturity by having survived both nature's limitations and many hunting seasons. The pursuit of such an animal limits the hunter's chances of taking an animal because there are few of them in a population. Testing your skill as a hunter by restricting yourself to the pursuit of these uncommon, individual animals elevates your personal standard. In this context, seeking a trophy is consistent with a sensitive hunting ethic.

Implicit in the idea "trophy" is that the game pursued is a wild, free-ranging animal and that other hunters have not been completely restricted from its pursuit. Also implicit in the trophy concept is that the animal is the natural product of the land. Practices such as stimulating antler growth with mineral blocks, hormones, or other substances is beyond acceptable ethical practice, and diminishes the value of all trophies.

The Ethical Pursuit of Trophy

The ethics of pursuing a trophy animal are closely tied to why we seek such an animal. If you hunt these animals because they represent the survivors of many hunts, and you respect that achievement, then you have selected a high personal standard. If, on the other hand, you pursue a trophy to establish that you, as an individual hunter, are superior to other hunters, then you have done it to enhance your personal status, and that crosses the ethical line. No animal should be killed for that reason.

Hunting is not a contest between humans. Trophy scoring and big game contests come perilously close to, and sometimes cross, the line of proper ethical practice. In other words, trying to take a trophy to get your name in a record book is taking a fine animal for the wrong reason. Contests between hunters that require killing animals should be prohibited. Trying to kill the "big buck" to win a contest or a monetary prize also represents pursuing and killing wildlife for the wrong reasons.

The idea of hunting trophy animals and the preservation of wildlife have a deep and common root in our history. One of our nation's oldest and proudest conservation organizations has done both well for over a century. There is value in keeping trophy records, and they should include information about the animal, the land that produced it, and the wild nature of the habitat that sustained it. Over time, valuable information about a species and the land is collected and preserved. Displaying the name of the hunter, however, may no longer be necessary.

Living With a Trophy

Human perceptions of grace, strength, beauty, and edibility—along with the necessities of subsistence—contributed to the notion of game animals. For the hunter, the display of a trophy is a reminder of the hunt and a way of extending the appreciation of the experience and the animal.

In this respect every animal ever taken is a trophy. They are all things of beauty and remembering them through photography, taxidermy, or other forms of art is reasonable.

The following is a story of two trophy mule deer bucks and how a hunter perceives their value and his achievement in taking them.

⫷⫸⫷

The Old Bucks of Wolf Creek

The slope above Wolf Creek is steep and cloud-piercing. It is a spot where a mountainous wild place crashes into a deep valley, and big game come there to escape deep snow. In 1955 a college student spent an entire morning climbing the Wolf Creek slope to get above a huge mule deer buck he had spotted at first light. In early afternoon, the buck fell. Later the young hunter stopped at a taxidermist who told him to have the head mounted. He added, "You will never kill another buck like it."

A year later the same hunter took an enormous buck in the foothills at the base of the same slope. The taxidermist was correct, but only by a little. These two magnificent animals were fully mature male deer. They came to the foothills of a wild and beautiful place to be in the company of does pushed there by the snow. One was shot after an arduous stalk along a high, open, wind-swept ridge. The other was taken early on a frigid morning when deep powder snow and the buck's ardor gave a break to the young hunter.

These two magnificent deer still adorn the walls of the hunter's home. The judgment of the taxidermist has held up, although the hunter goes afield each year and has taken many deer since the two monarchs fell. The truth is that the hunter has not seen another buck the equal of either.

As the years passed, the hunter began to appreciate the significance of these bucks and all the people that had to care about wildlife and wild places in order to bring these trophies to his wall. He also came to realize these trophies were products of a time when the country was wilder, and the bucks, secure in that wildness, got old. The hunter didn't know these facts when he shot the bucks, but he knows and appreciates these things now. The hunter also knows that these massive deer were not, and are not, a testament to his prowess as a hunter. He knows they were and are a testament to the land and to its ability to produce truly marvelous animals if given the chance.

These two fine sets of antlers are still with the

hunter after almost forty years. He doesn't know what those antlers would "score" if their length and girth were measured in inches and fractions of inches. Those numbers would have no meaning to trophies that are in all ways a product of a place and a time. You cannot measure nutrition, solitude, wildness, and a decade or more of passing seasons in inches or even feet. So it is that the hunter has never laid a measuring tape against those heavy, long, graceful beams—and never will.

THE NORTH
AMERICAN HUNTER

The Hunter-Conservationist

There would be no hunting if there were no wild animals. The fact that there would be few wild animals if there were no hunters is not as obvious. Both of these statements are true, and they are things everyone should know about the American hunter/conservationist.

When North America was settled, any resource that could be made useful was taken. That was true for water, land, minerals, trees, and wildlife. Wildlife was useful for food and clothing, so people took what was available. As the number of people grew, wildlife declined. The following statements were made early in the twentieth century:

"It may be confidently asserted that twenty-five years hence, the rinderpest (a viral disease) and repeating rifle will have destroyed most, if not all the larger ...fauna, and game in ... North America in a wild state will almost have ceased to exist." (Madison Grant, 1904)

"... all the 'old-timers' agreed that there are no Antelope in the country now."
(Ernest Thompson Seton, 1909)

"It seems as if all the killable game of North America, except rabbits, is now being crushed to death between the upper millstone of industries and trade, and the ... lower millstone made up by the killers of wildlife." (William T. Hornaday)

During this bleak time, someone had to step forward and speak for wildlife if game animals and hunting were going to survive to our generation. The truth is, the sportsmen and women of that era had already begun to give wildlife a voice. As early as 1871 sport hunters were speaking out for wildlife. One historian noted:

"The appearance of a new monthly newspaper, the *American Sportsman*, in October, 1871 marks a watershed in environmental history." (John F. Rieger)

"With the appearance of national periodicals like *American Sportsman* (1871), *Field and Stream* (1874), and *American Angler* (1881), a new impetus was given to the sportsmen's struggle against commercial exploitation of wildlife." (John F. Rieger)

An interesting fact about conservation history should be noted. The United States observed the first "Earth Day" in 1970. This "day" marked the time when the general public recognized it was time to stop destroying nature. Yet as early as 1871, nearly a century before Earth Day, hunters and anglers were speaking out for nature and the environment. There were many people who contributed to the conservation of wildlife, and all hunters have a responsibility to study this history. The references listed at the end of this book will get you started and make you proud to be a hunter.

The Evolution of the American Hunter

Human ideas, perceptions, and values are constantly evolving. At the same time, the natural world that produced us remains as important as ever. The natural world sustains us with clean air, unpolluted water, recreation, and natural resources. If we destroy nature, we destroy ourselves. Many of us return to nature through our recreation to learn and to be re-created.

For those of us who hunt, we return as hunters. As hunters we enjoy the rare privilege of participating in the natural process rather than only observing it from a distance. We become, for a time, a predator like the human hunters of our distant origins. We are, however, a minority; and if we are to continue, we must do it in a way that is acceptable to the majority. These people do not hunt, but they support the ethical pursuit of wildlife.

We defined an ethical hunter as:

A person who knows and respects the animals hunted, follows the law, and behaves in a way that will satisfy what society expects of him or her as a hunter.

This definition recognized that we must be responsive to what the rest of the people think about hunting and hunters. Hunting is a primal activity. It is an activity that we find rewarding and re-creating. We must remember, however, that in our modern world each generation is more removed from nature. Each generation has fewer personal experiences with, and an understanding of, nature. If hunting is going to be acceptable in a changing society, we must address change and our own evolution as hunters.

What critics of hunting find objectionable are:

⬦ unethical hunter behavior,
⬦ killing only for trophy, and
⬦ killing for fun.

Aspects of hunting that are seen as positive are:

⬦ hunting for food,
⬦ hunting to manage wildlife populations,

◇ hunting as a way of appreciating nature through participation, and

◇ the conservation achievements of hunters.

The ideas presented in this book are offered to encourage change by emphasizing what is positive. The direction for change suggests nurturing a deep respect for the animals we hunt and the hunting environment. Cultivating a profound respect for wildlife and the land will affect how we behave as hunters, how we act as citizen conservationists, and how the public perceives us. That, in turn, will affect what happens to the land, and it is the land, as wild as we can sustain it, that both the hunter and the hunted need to survive.

RECOMMENDED READING AND STUDY

American Sportsmen and the Origins of Conservation, by John F. Reiger. University of Oklahoma Press. 1986, 316pp.

An American Crusade for Wildlife, by James B. Trefethen. Boone and Crockett Club. 1975, 409pp.

The History of Wildlife in America, by Hal Borland. National Wildlife Federation. 1975, 197pp.

International Bowhunter Education Manual. National Bowhunter Education Foundation, Route 6 Box 199, Murray , KY 42071, 1991, 74pp.

Restoring America's Wildlife, 1937-1987. United States Department of Interior, Fish and Wildlife Service. 1987, 394pp.

Sand County Almanac, by Aldo Leopold. Oxford University Press. 1949, 226pp.

Bloodties - Nature, Culture, and the Hunt, by Ted Kerasote. Random House Inc., New York. 1993, 277pp.

A Hunter's Pledge, by The Izaak Walton League of America, 707 Conservation Lane, Gaithersburg, MD 20878-2983, Attn. Earl Hower, Director of Membership, (301) 548-0150.

ABOUT THE AUTHOR

Jim Posewitz founded Orion—The Hunters Institute in 1993 after a 32-year career as a biologist with the Montana Department of Fish, Wildlife & Parks. He led the agency's ecological program for fifteen years, and he has served on the boards of numerous conservation groups. His intense interest in the essence of the hunt and the history of the hunter-conservationist led to his appointment as an adjunct professor of history and philosophy at Montana State University. The university also presented him with its Blue-Gold Award for "distinguished services which have contributed to benefit mankind." He lives in Helena, Montana.

ABOUT ORION—
THE HUNTERS INSTITUTE

Orion—The Hunters Institute is a non-profit organization created to sustain hunting and resources essential to that purpose. National in scope, the institute works to assure ethical and responsible hunting. This effort begins with individual hunters, extends to agencies responsible for the environments in which hunting occurs, and includes those responsible for the public trust in fish and wildlife. For more information, write Orion—The Hunters Institute, P.O. Box 5088, Helena, Montana 59604, or call 406-449-2795.

USING *BEYOND FAIR CHASE* IN HUNTER EDUCATION PROGRAMS

Beyond Fair Chase can be used effectively in hunter education classes to teach hunter ethics and behavior. To encourage this educational program, discounts are available for books used in hunter education classes, and a teaching guide is available. The teaching guide contains complete lesson plans, dilemma cards, learning activities, and a test.

For more information please contact The Globe Pequot Press (1-800-243-0495) or Orion–The Hunters Institute (406-449-2795).

To order additional copies of this book, call toll-free at 1-800-243-0495. To order the hardcover edition of this book, please see your local bookstore or call or write to:

The Globe Pequot Press
P.O. Box 480
Guilford, Connecticut 06437